Oficial de Policía en Patrulla
Libro de colorear

Coloring Pages for Kids

**All rights reserved. No part of this document may be reproduced
Used or transmitted in any form or by any means, electronic or otherwise. This means you
cannot photocopy any material ideas or tips that are provided in this book.**

Coloring Pages for Kids
An imprint of Ciparum LLC

Oficial de Policía en Patrulla Libro de colorear
© 2017 Ciparum LLC
All rights reserved.
ISBN-10:1-63589-351-8
ISBN-13:978-1-63589-351-9

Coloring Pages for Kids

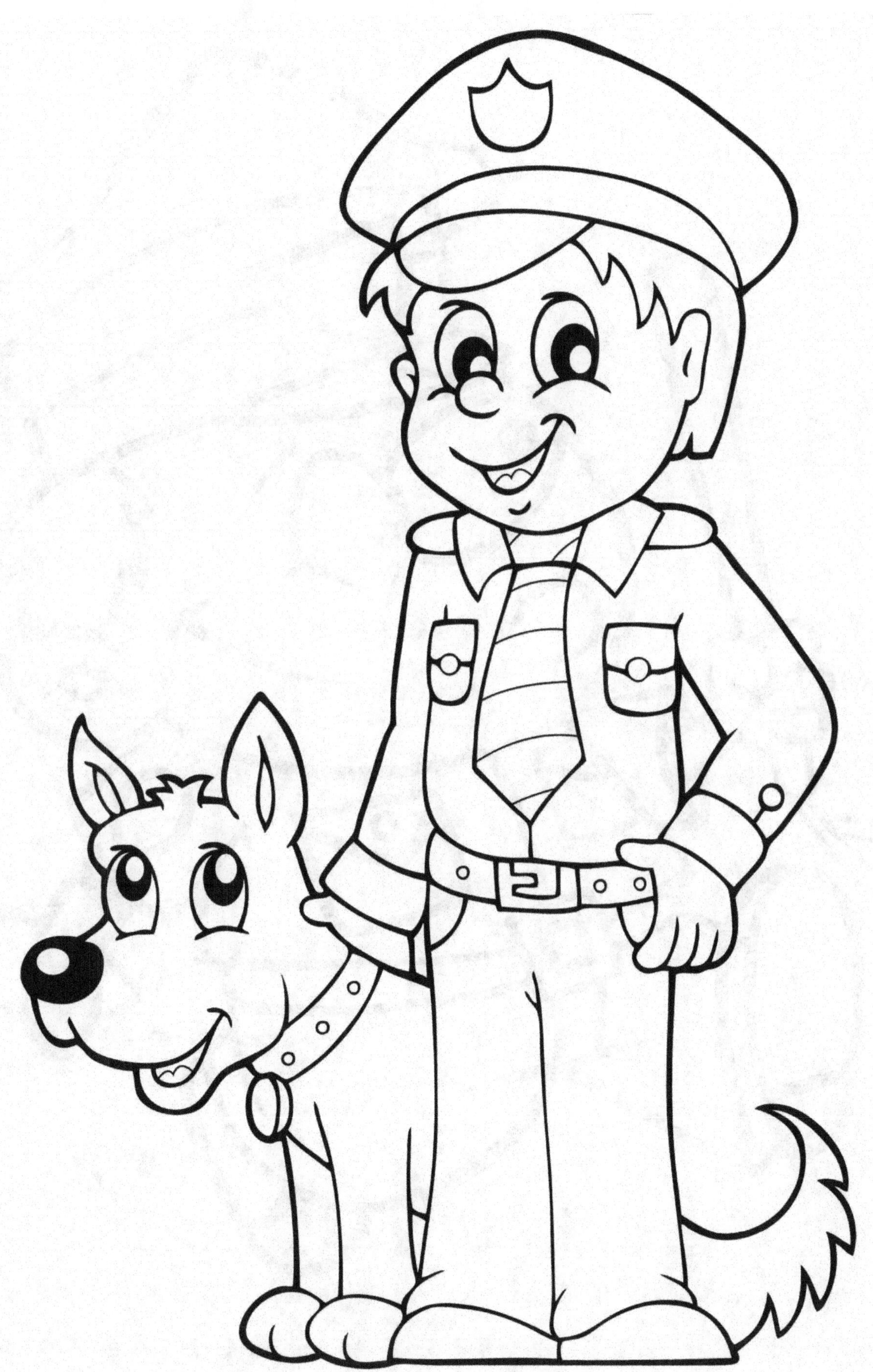

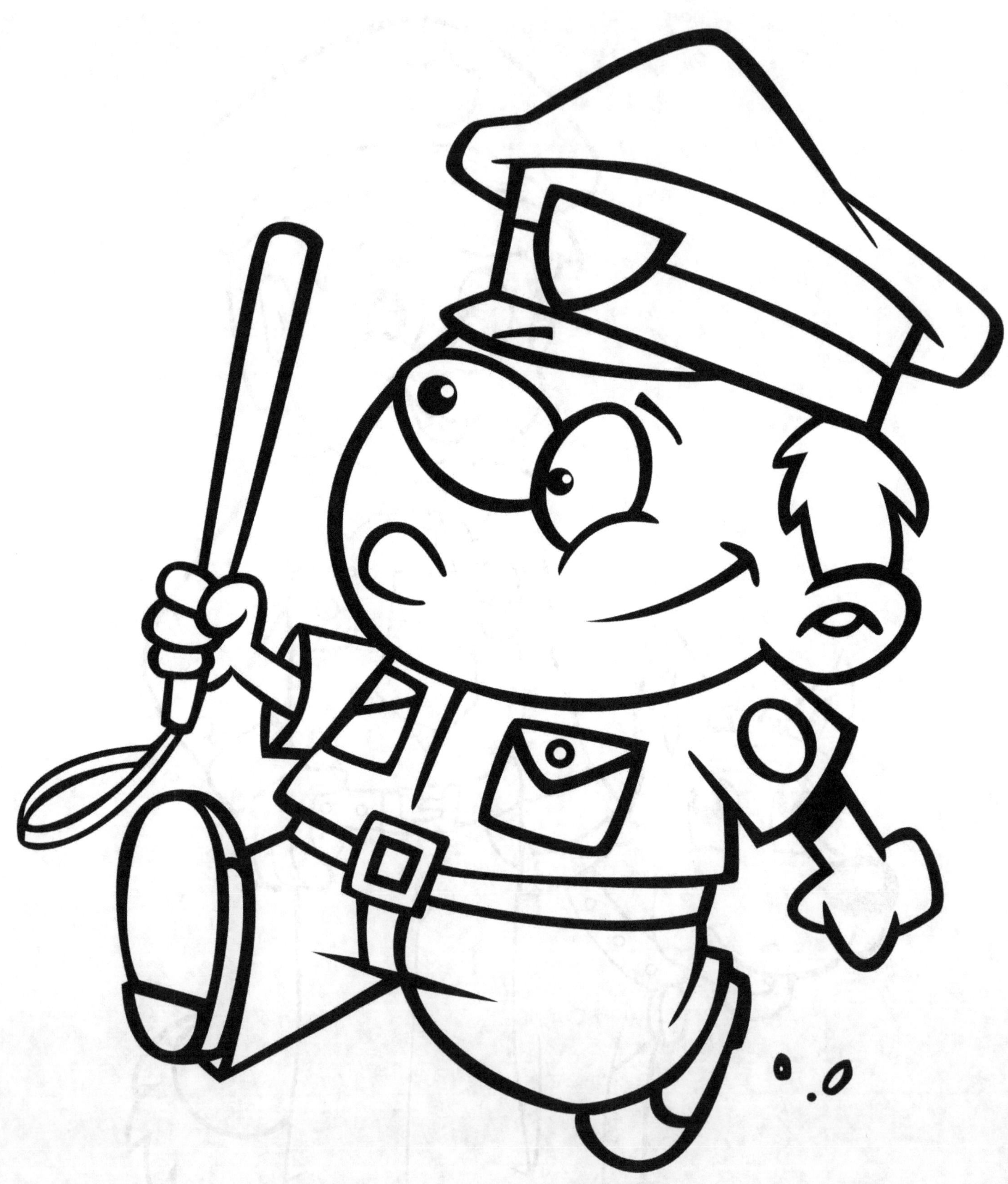

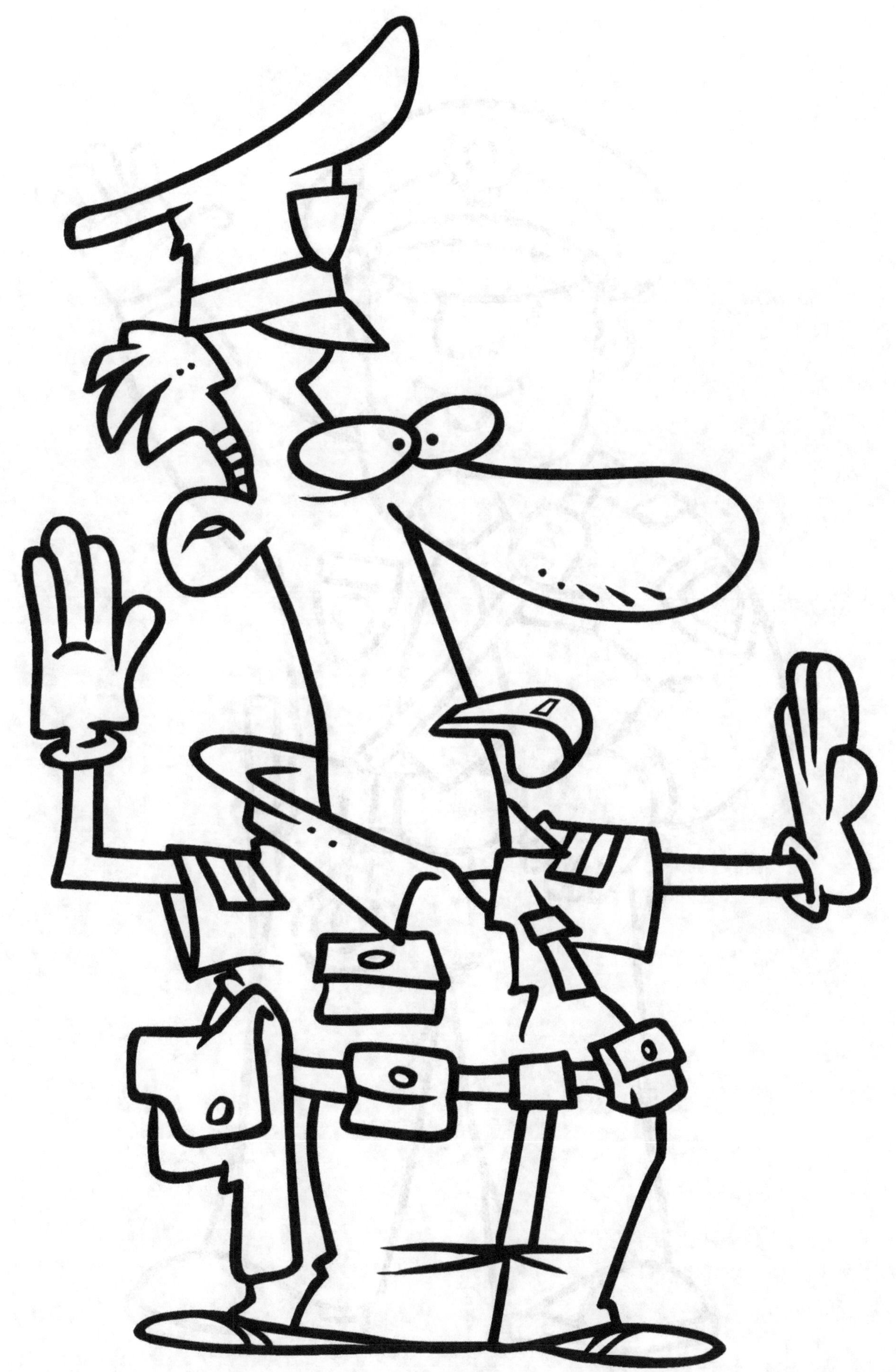

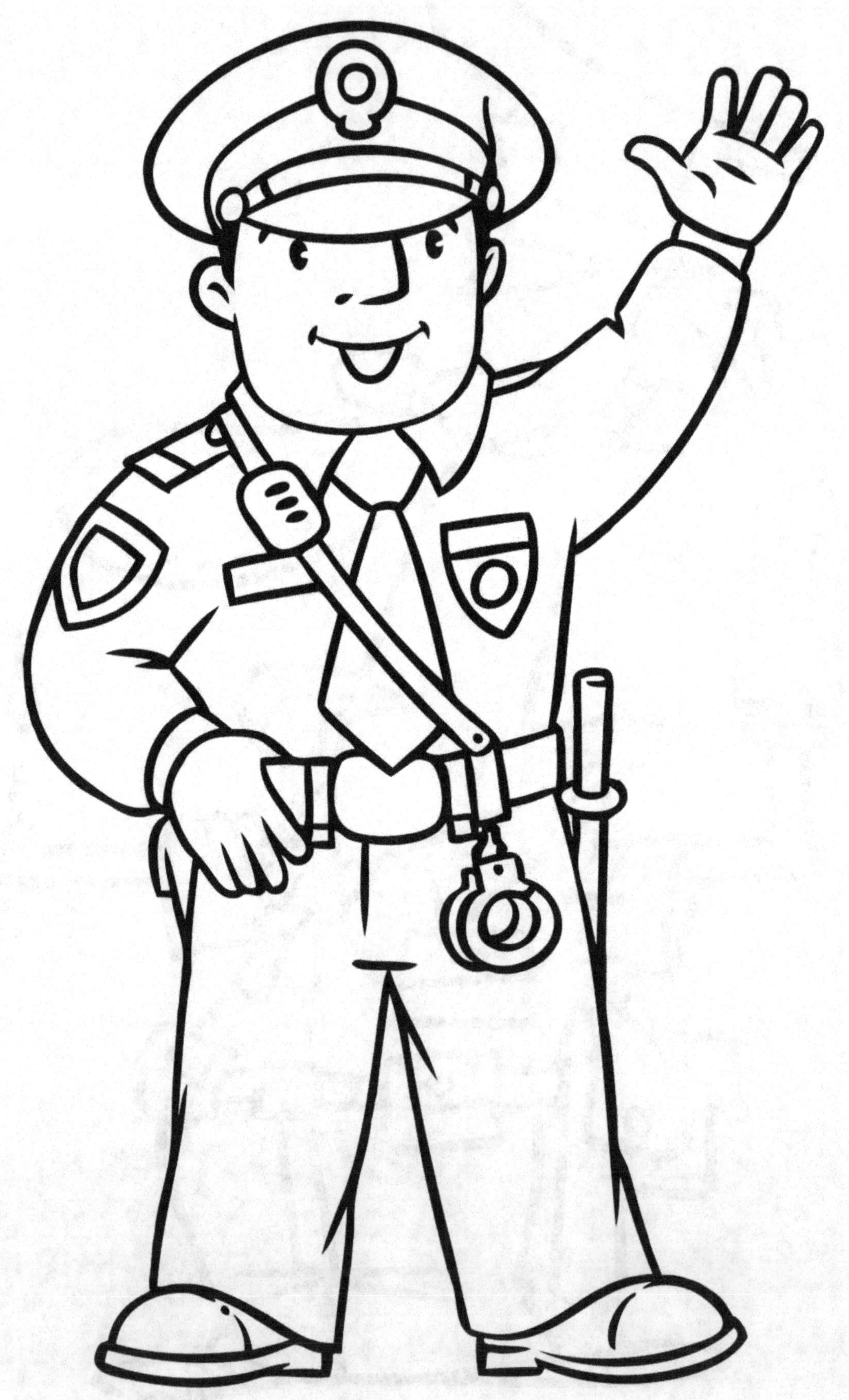

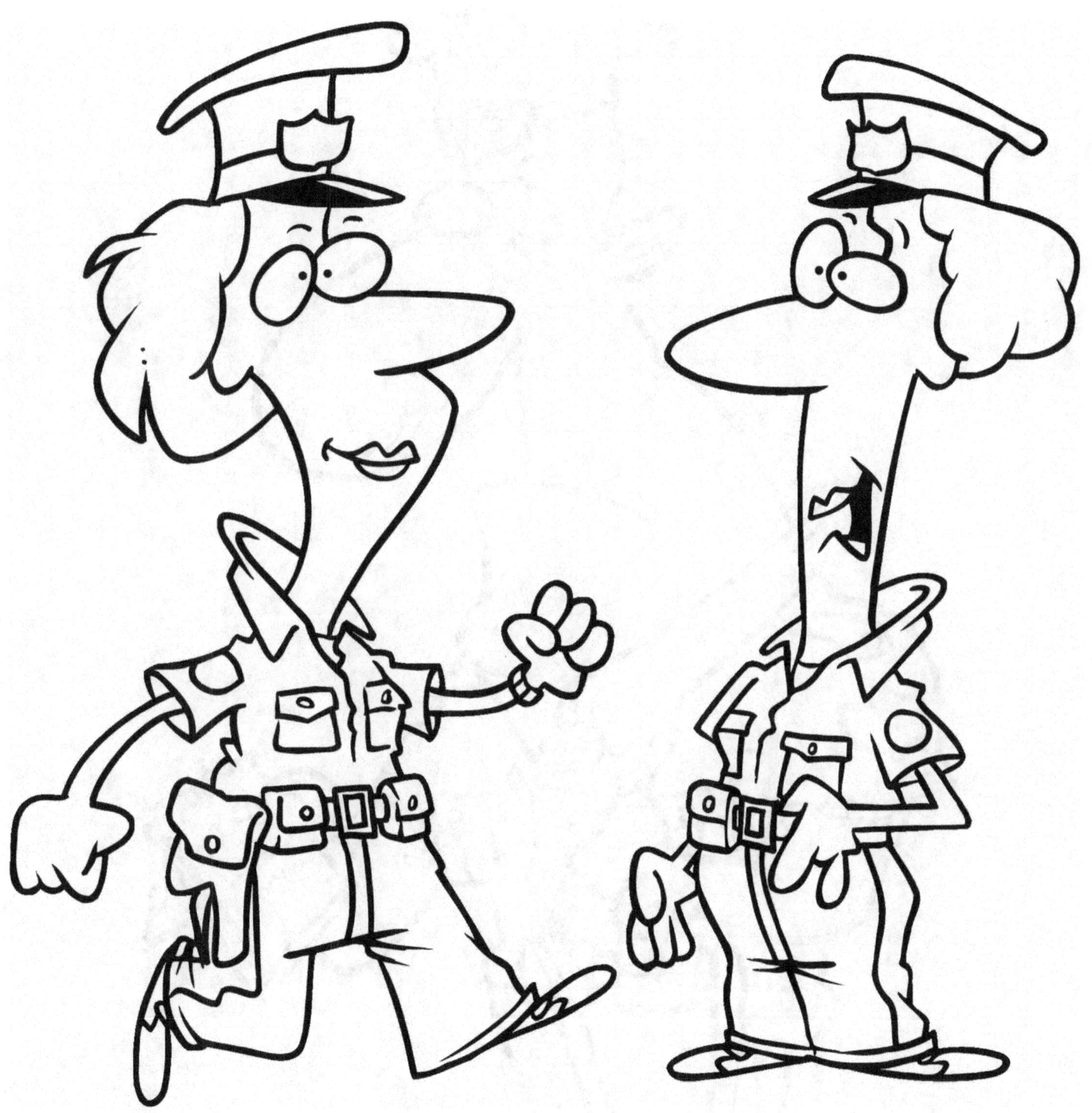

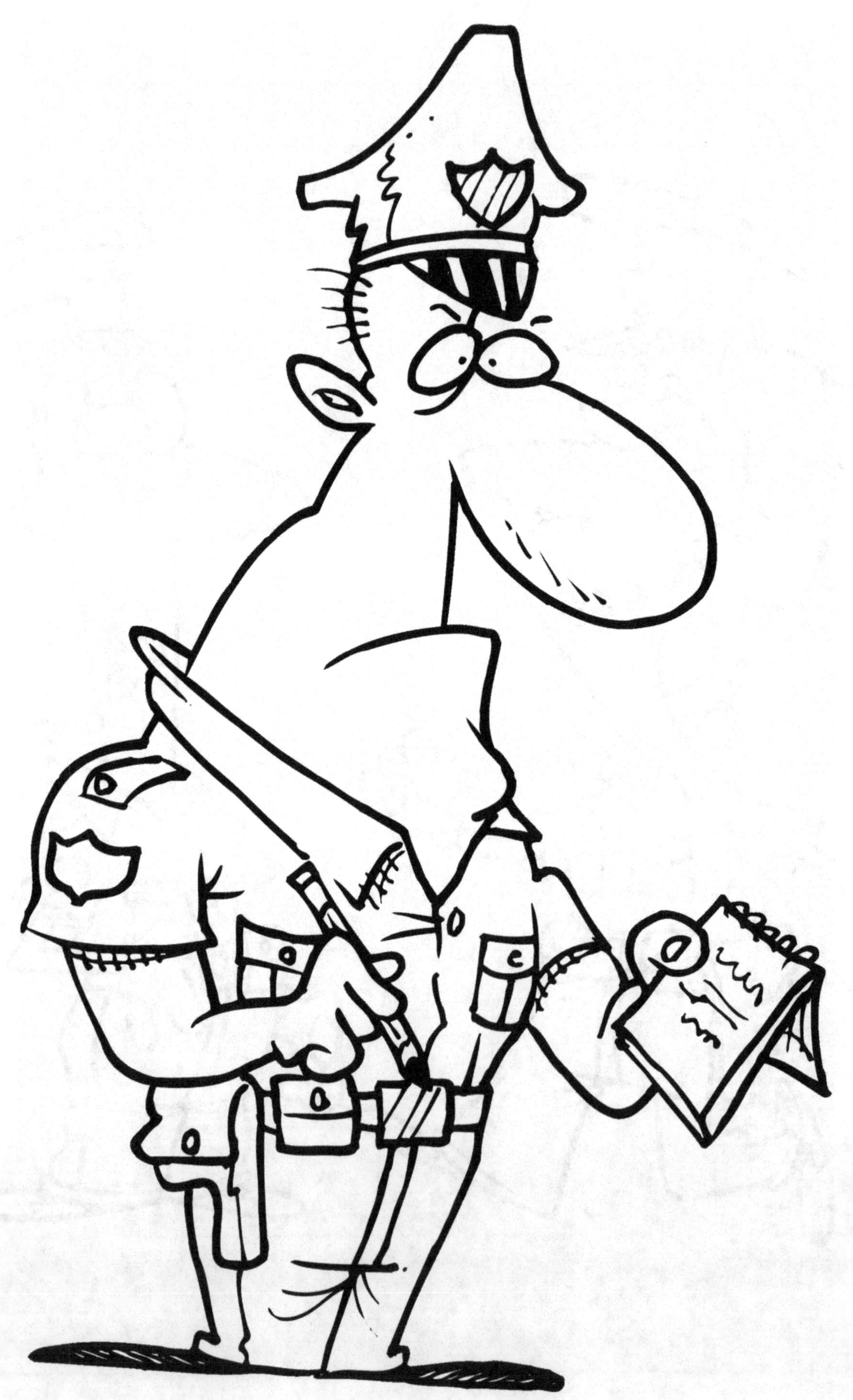

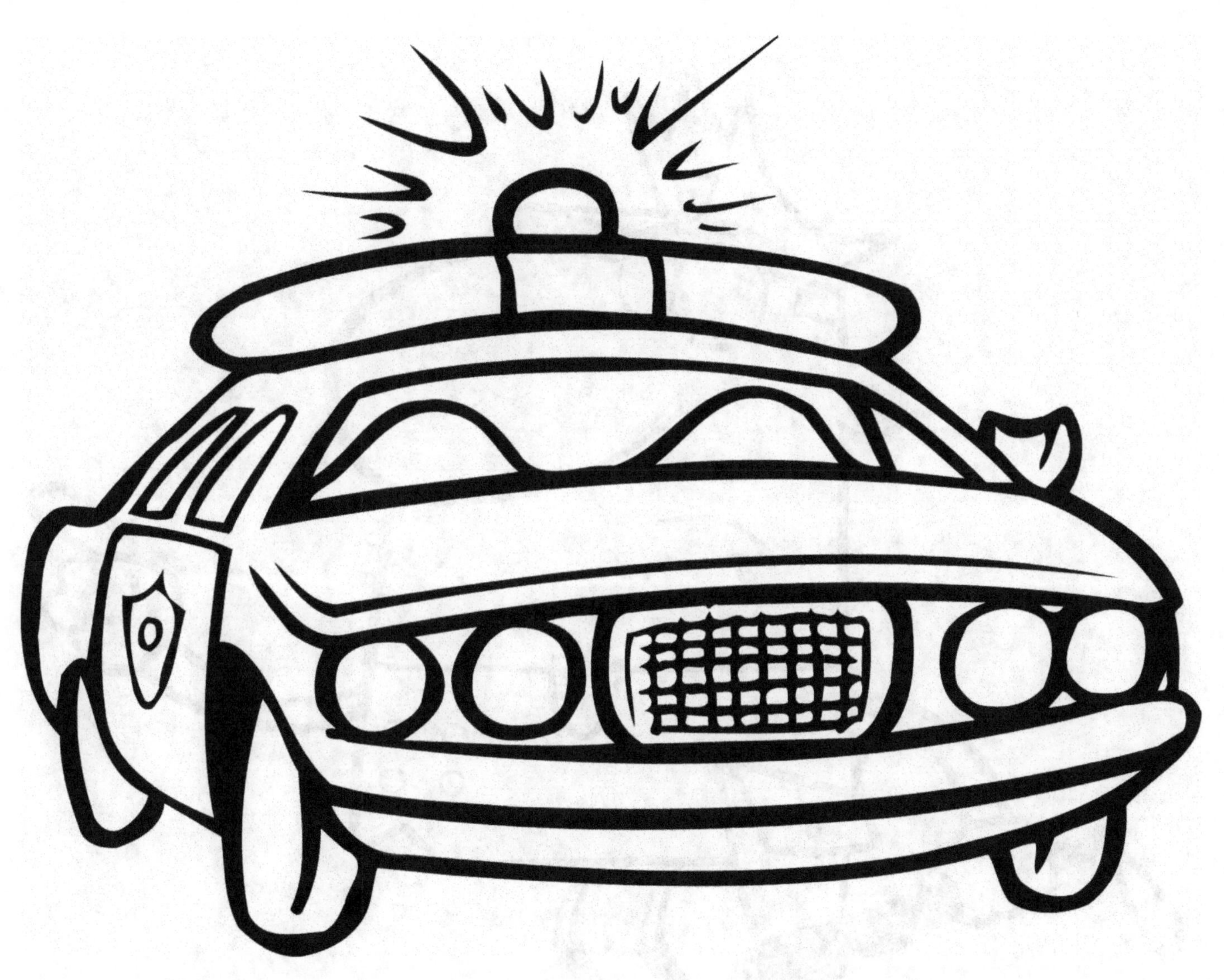

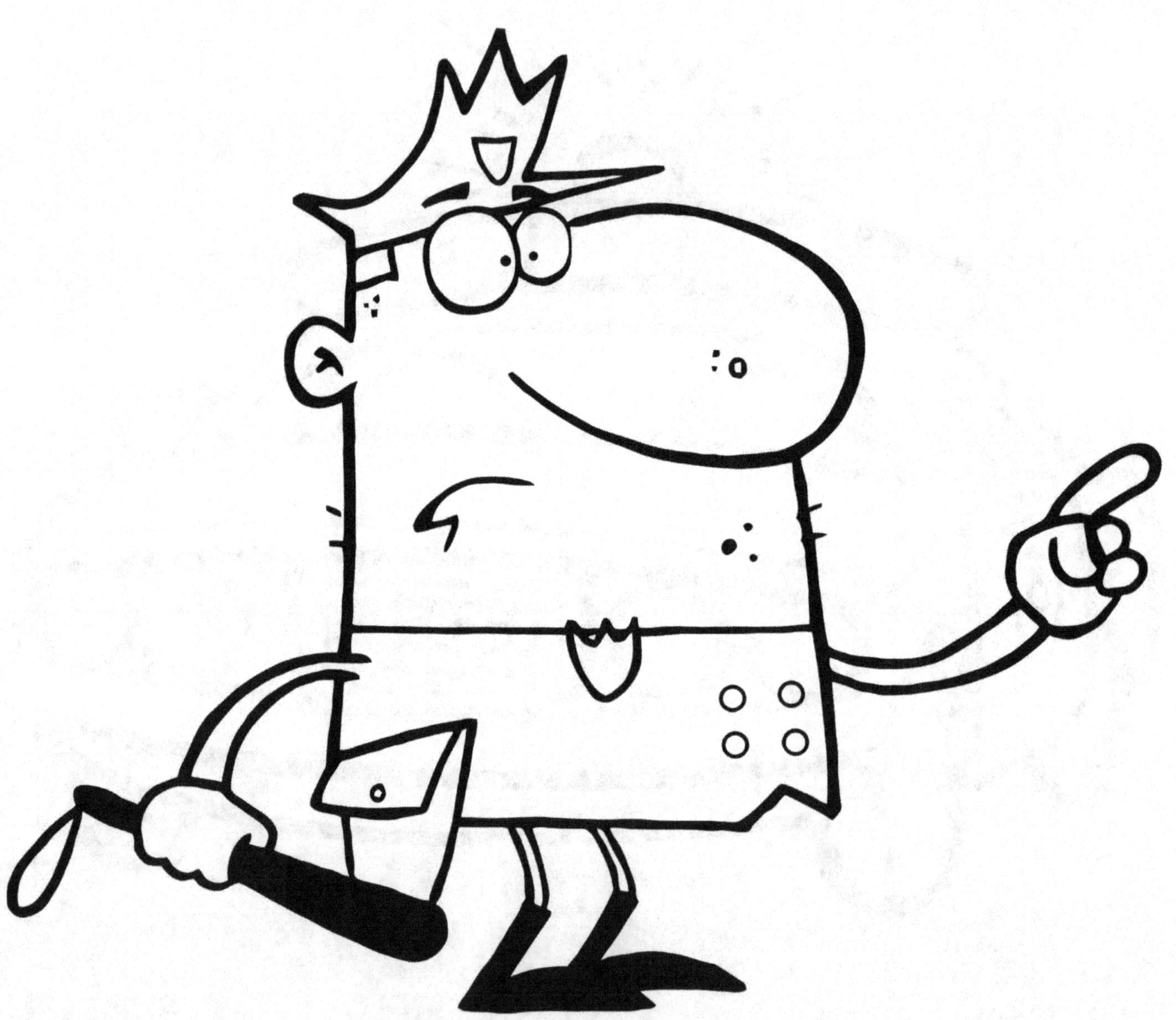

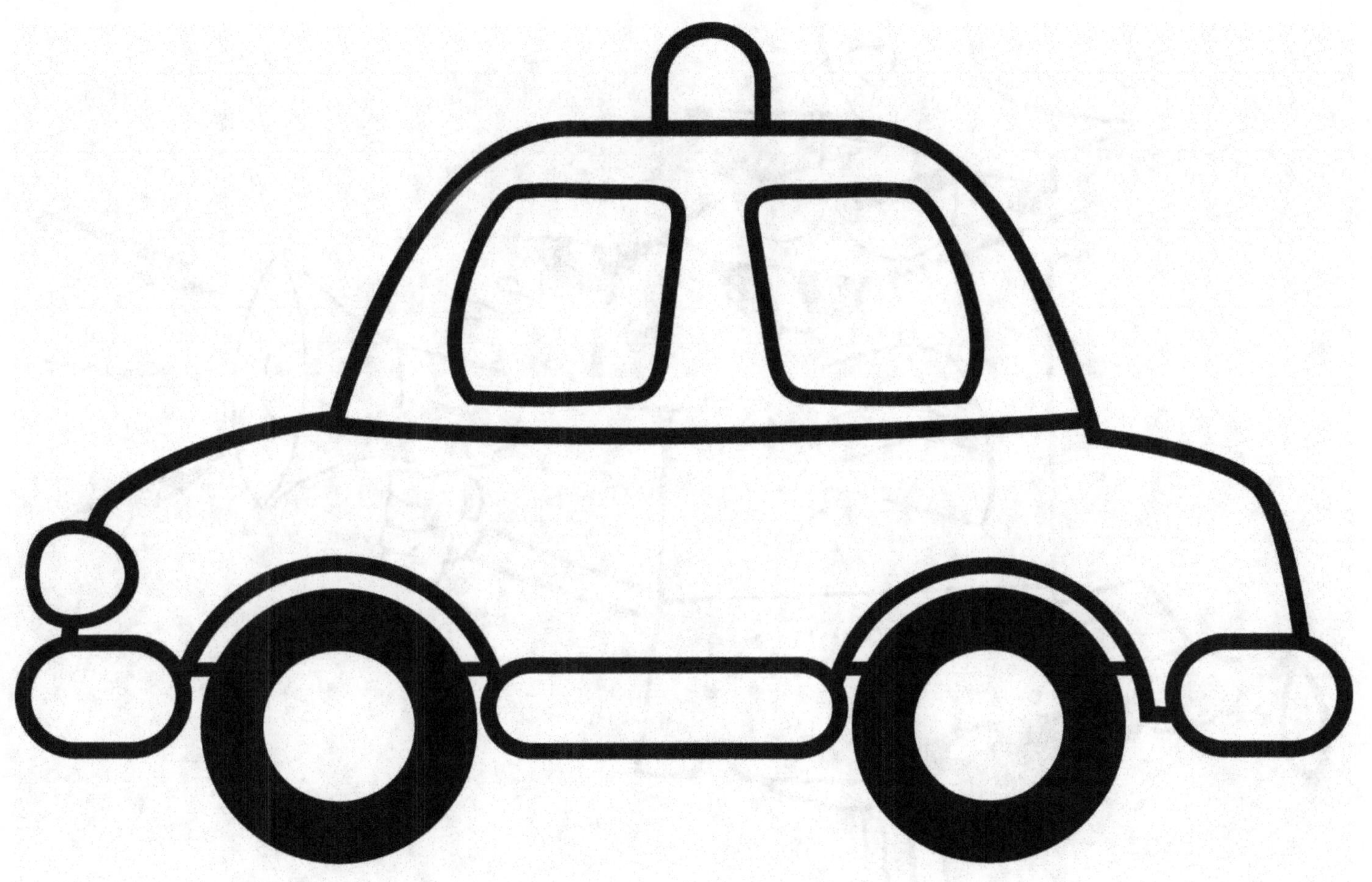

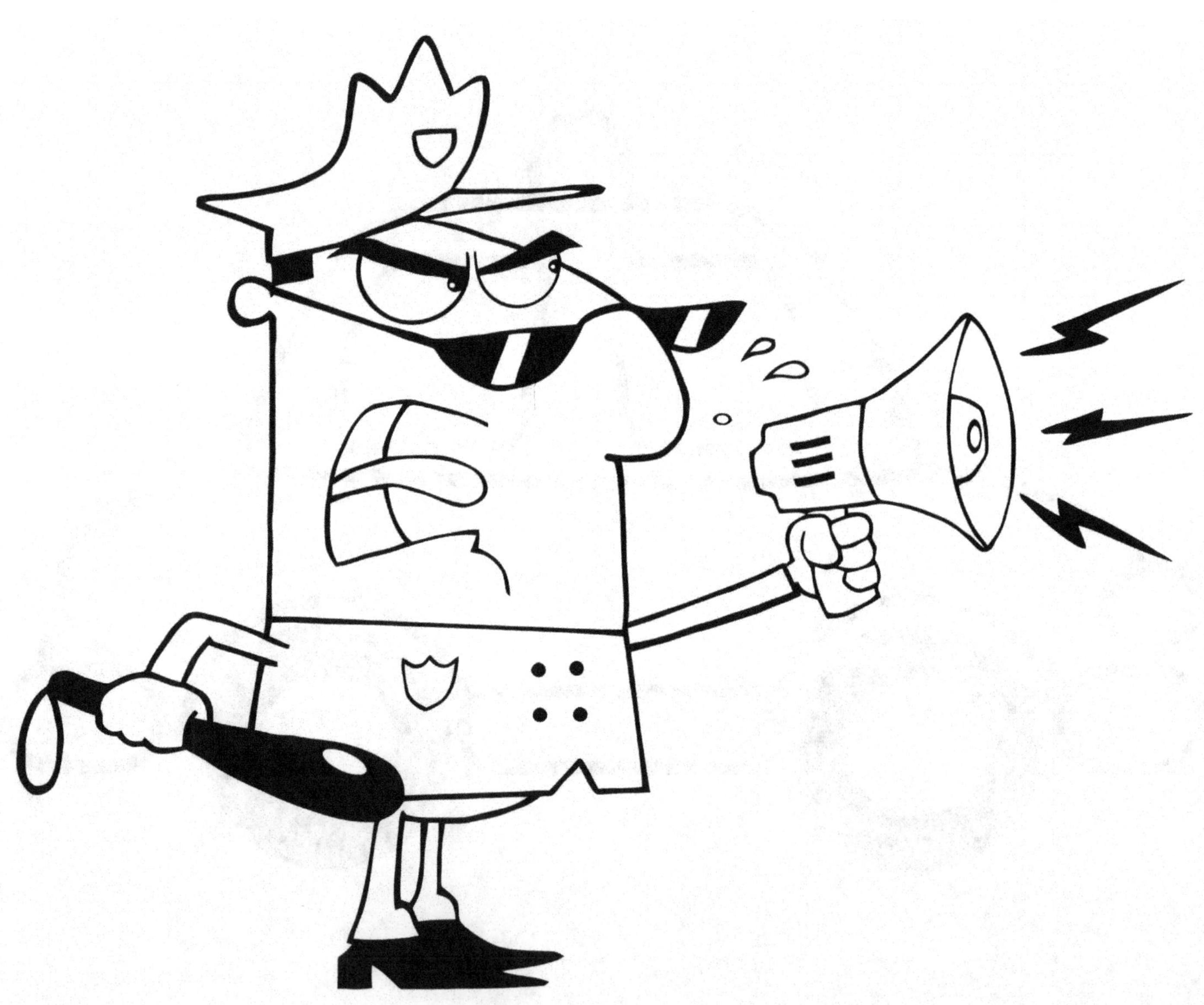

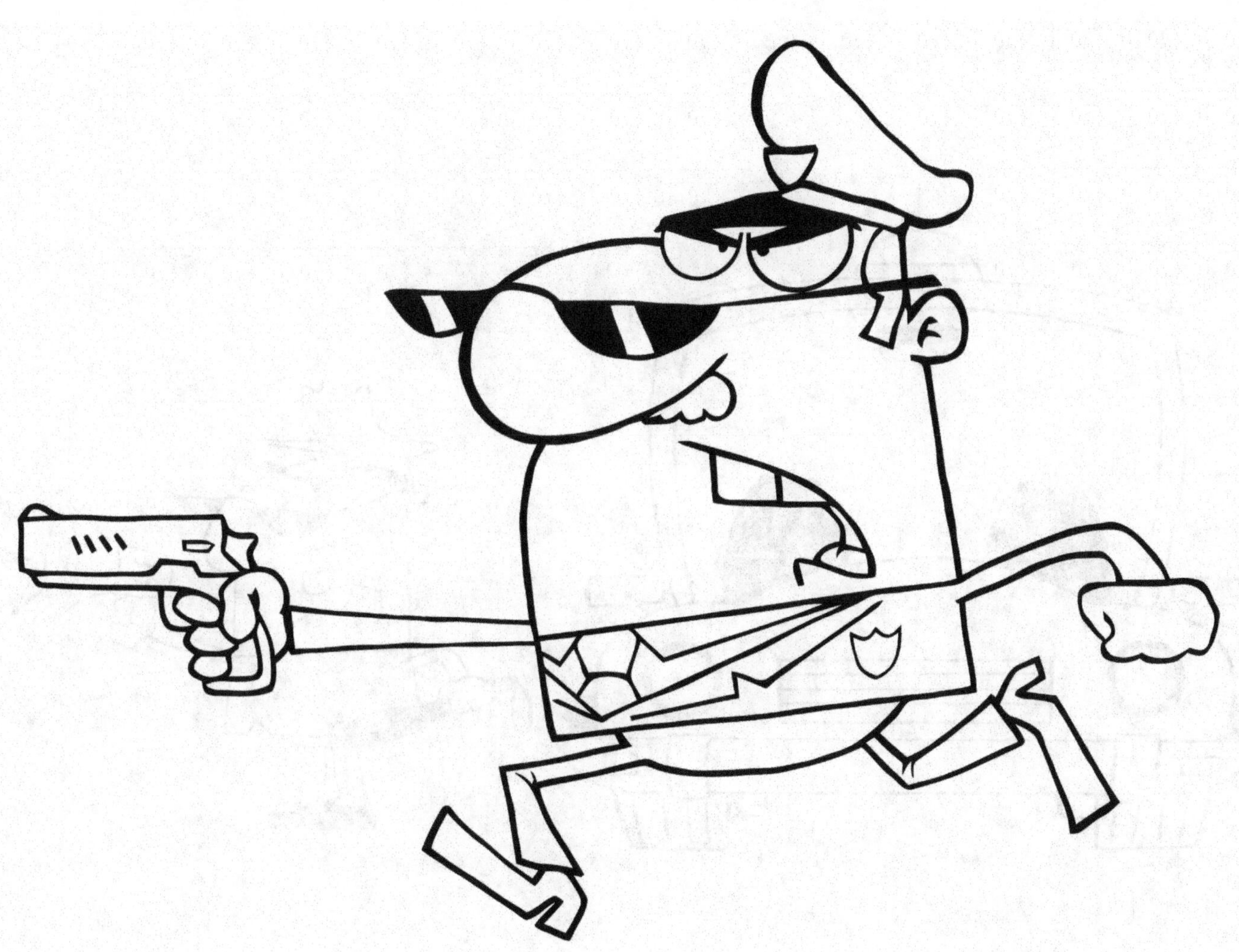

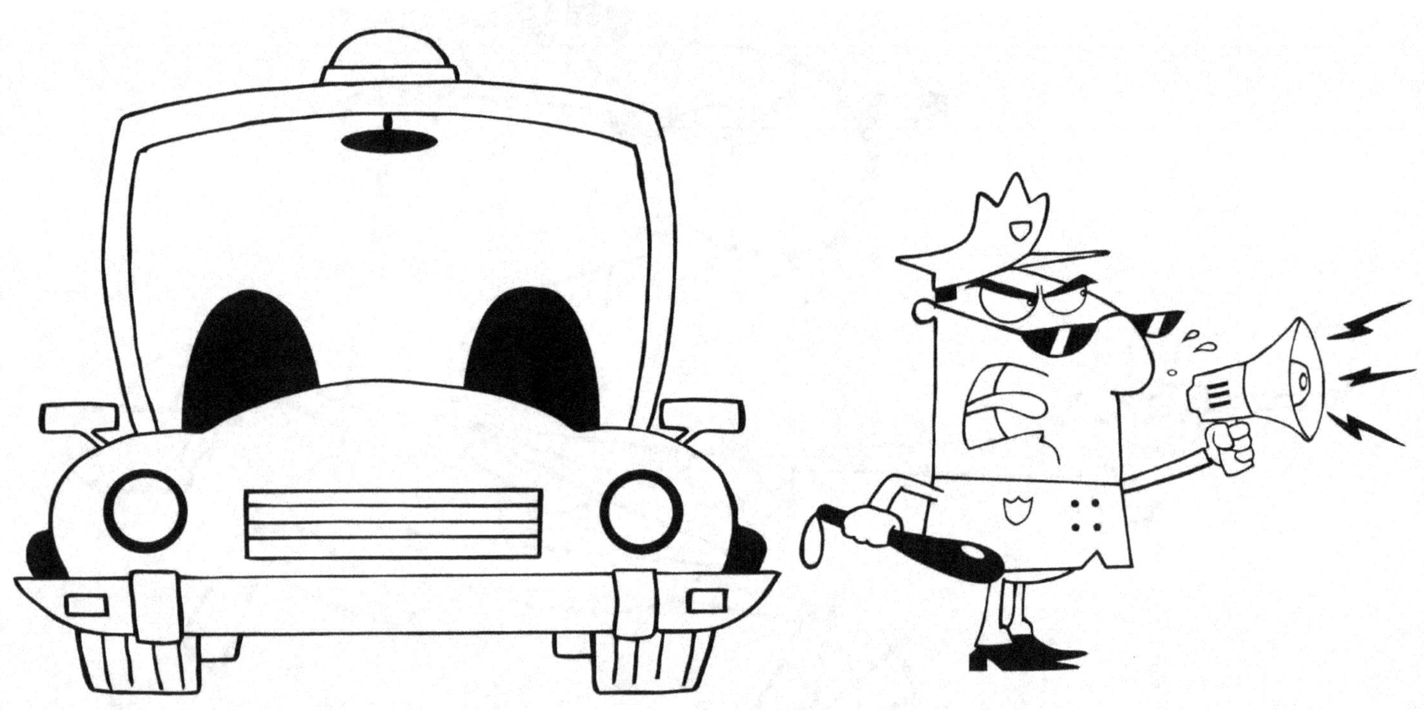

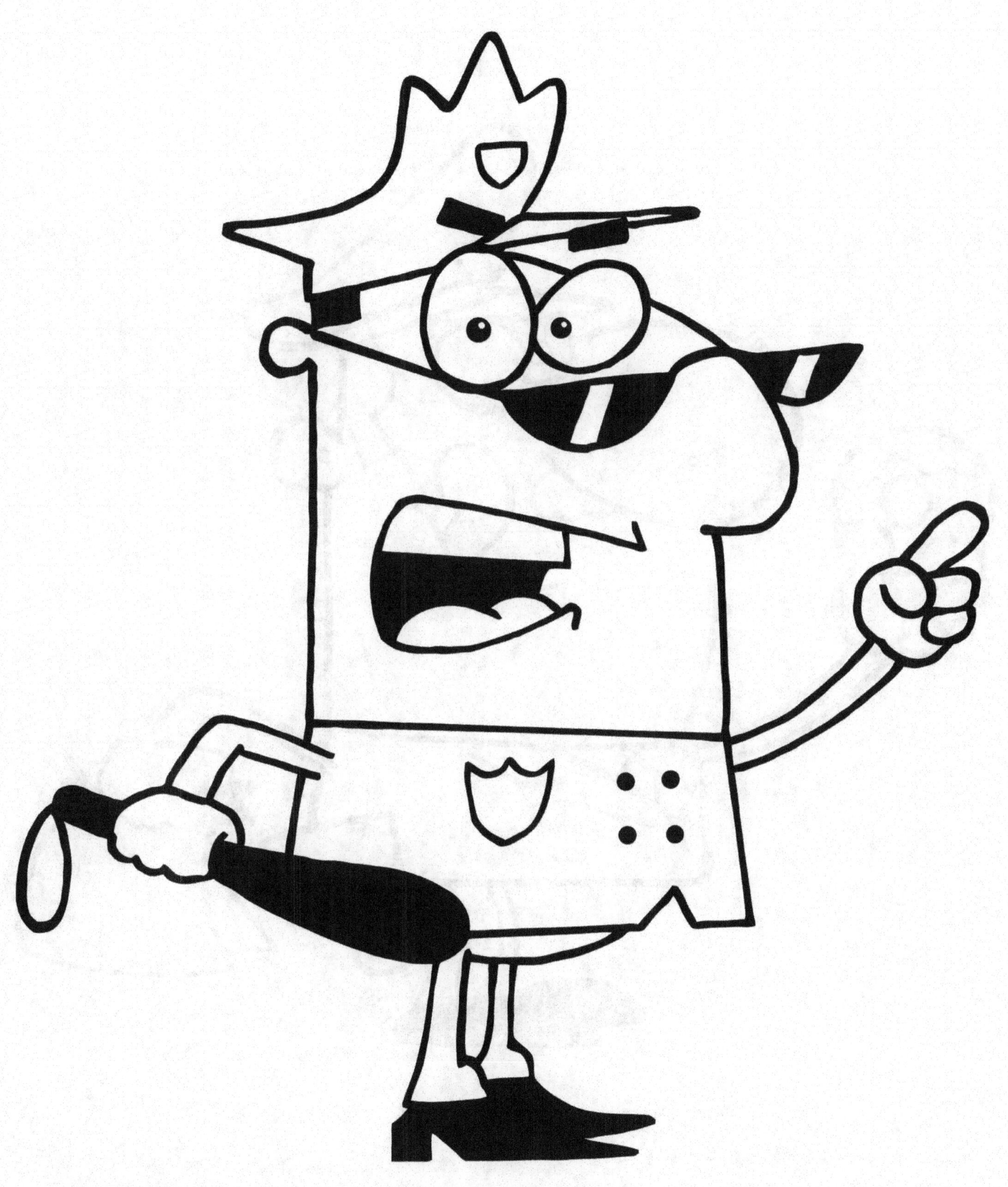

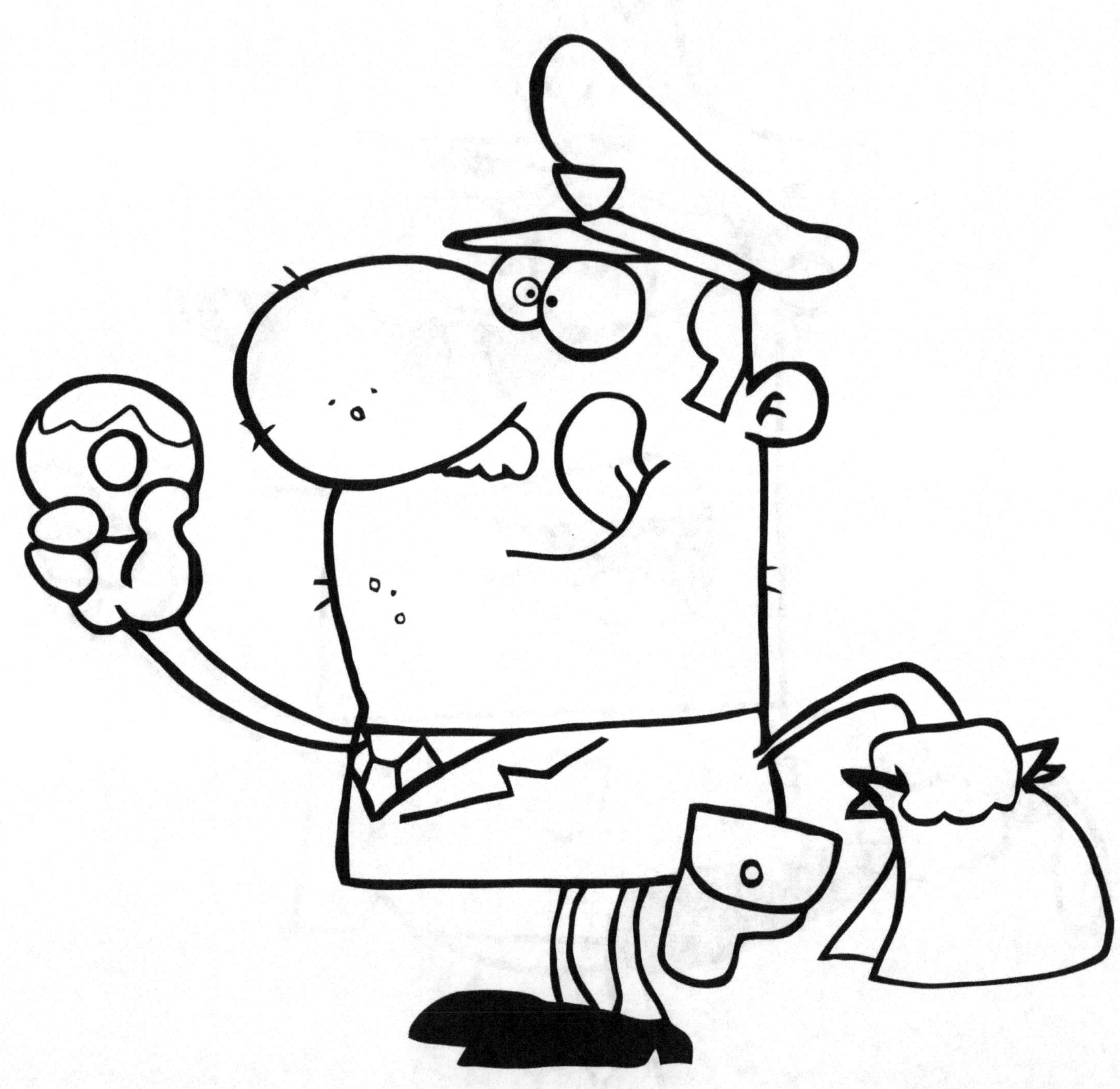

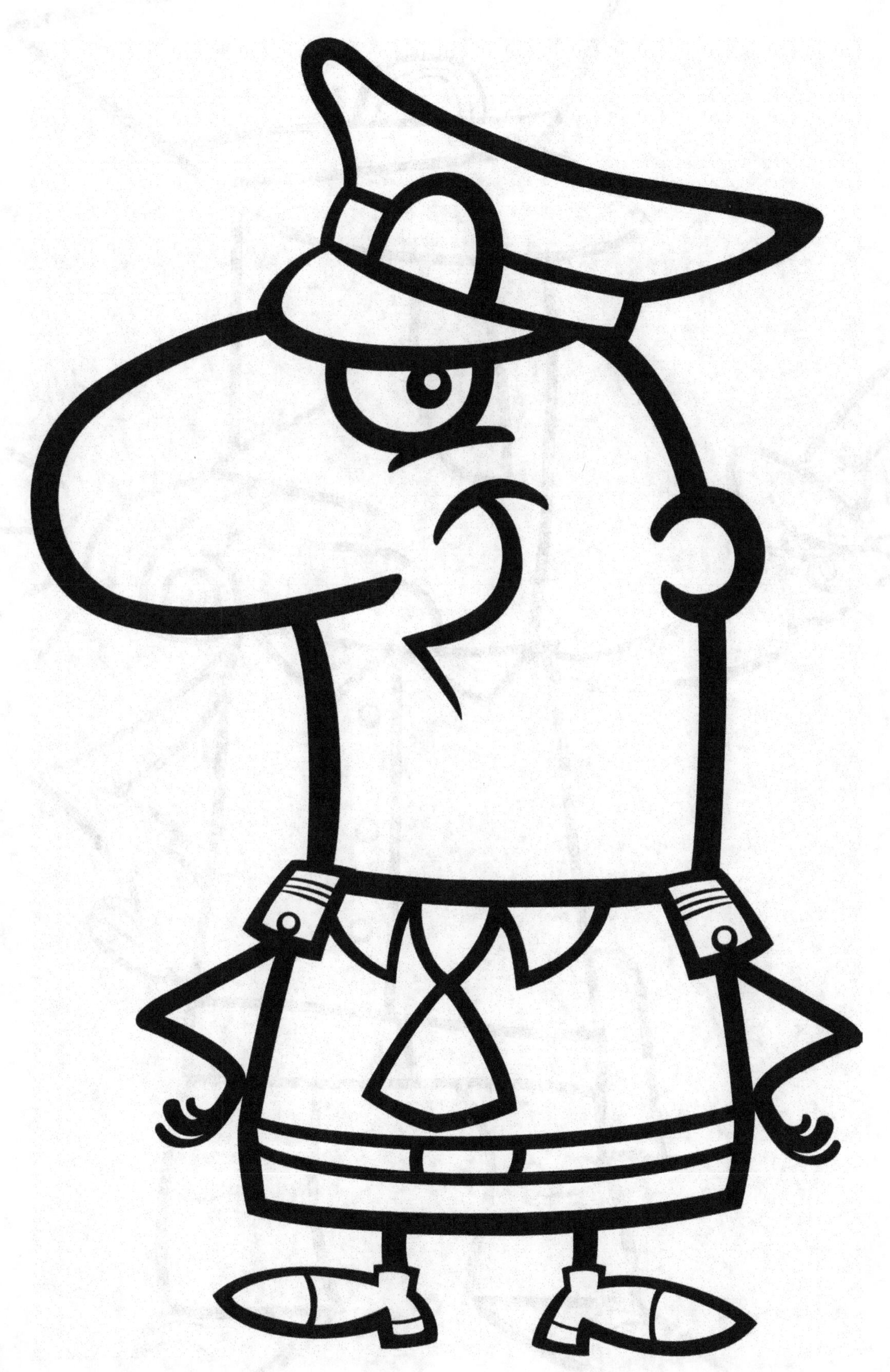

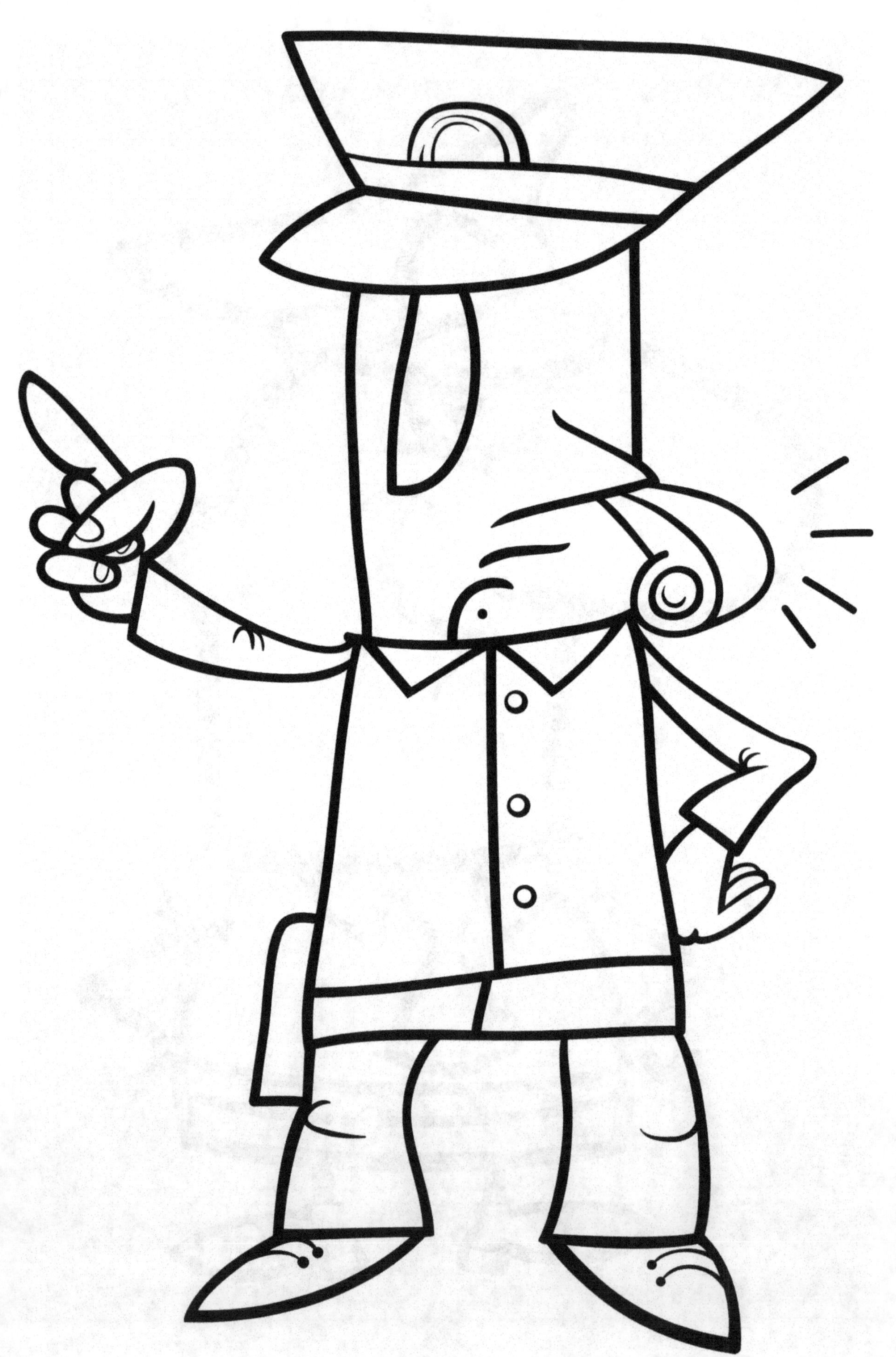

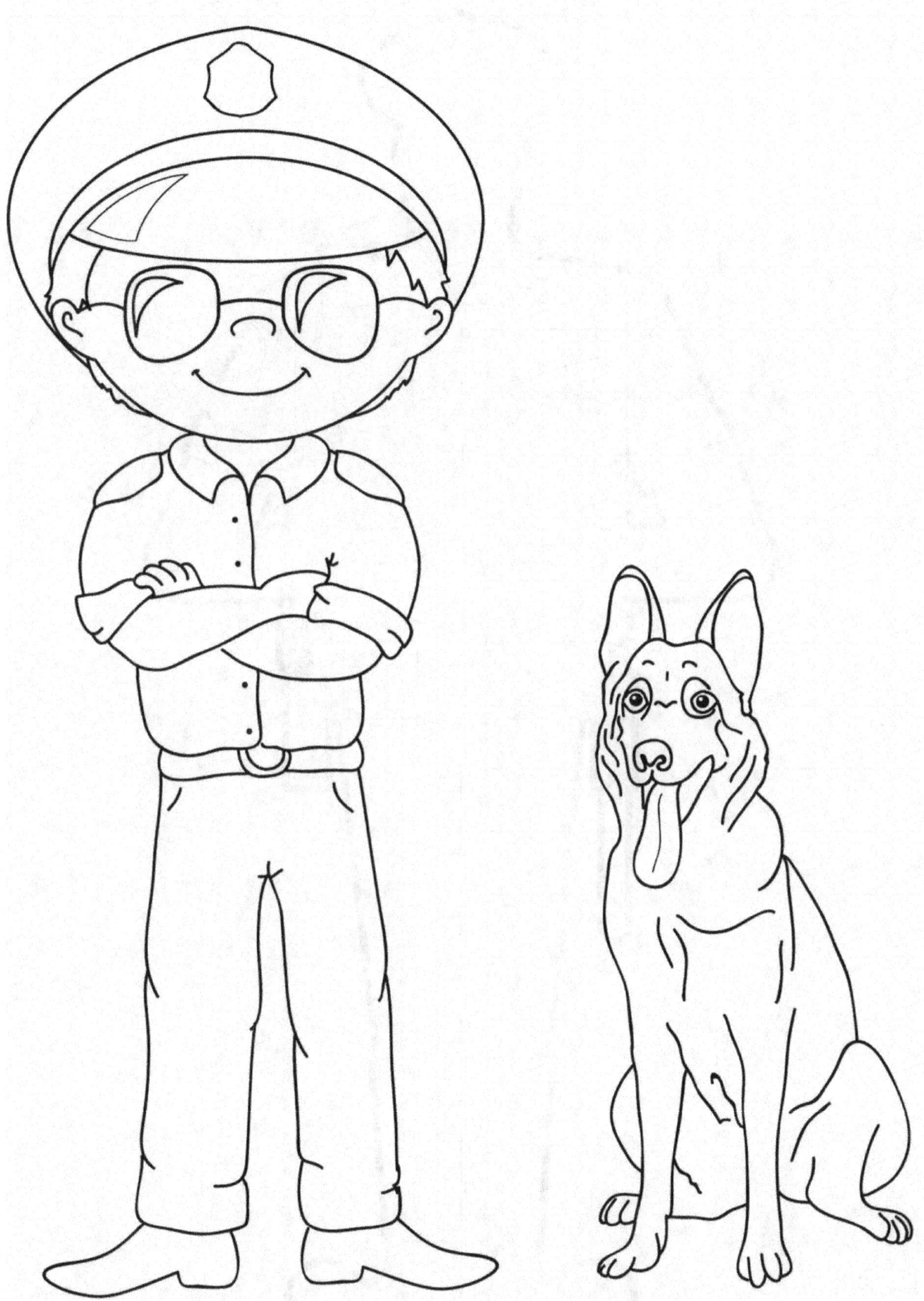

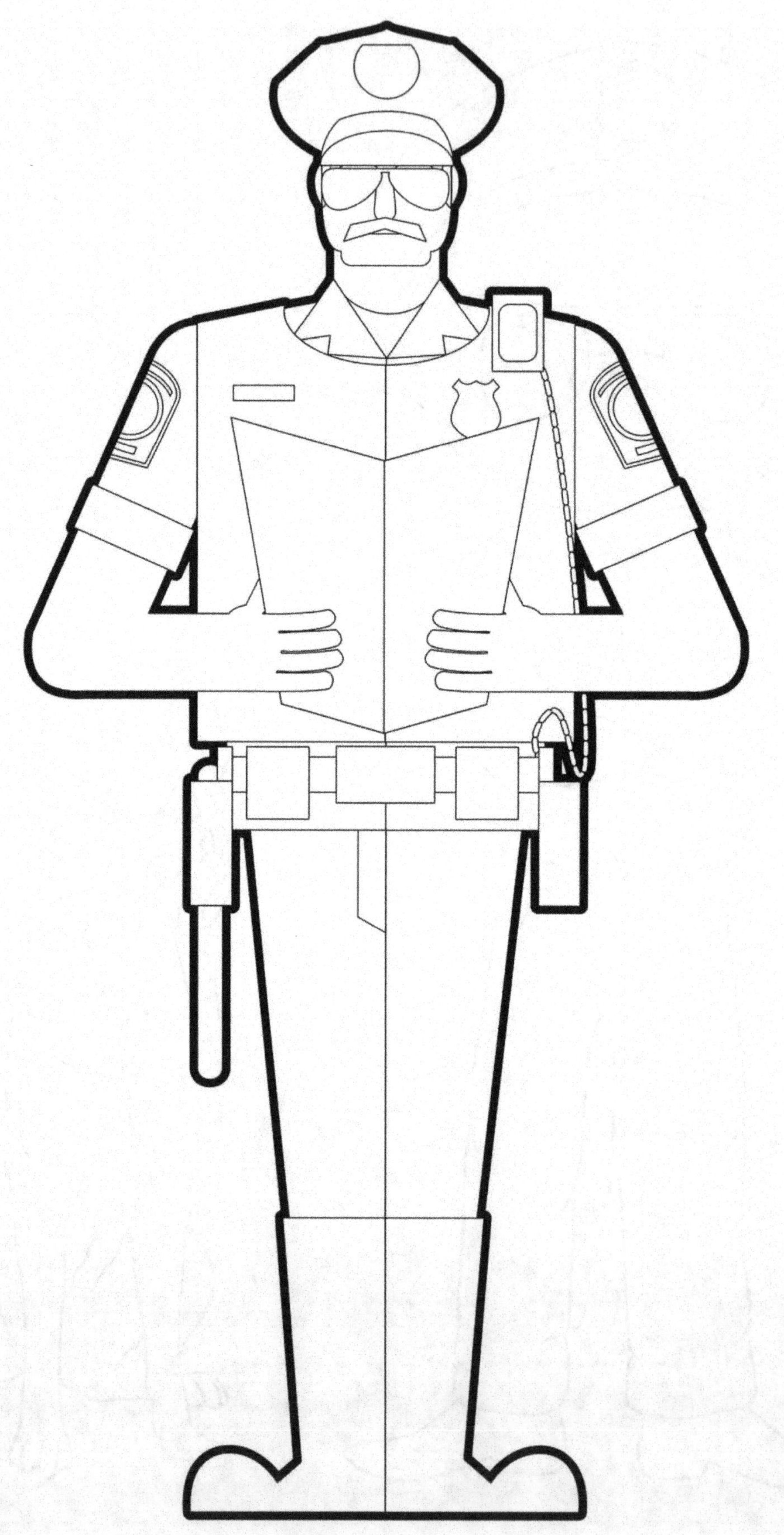

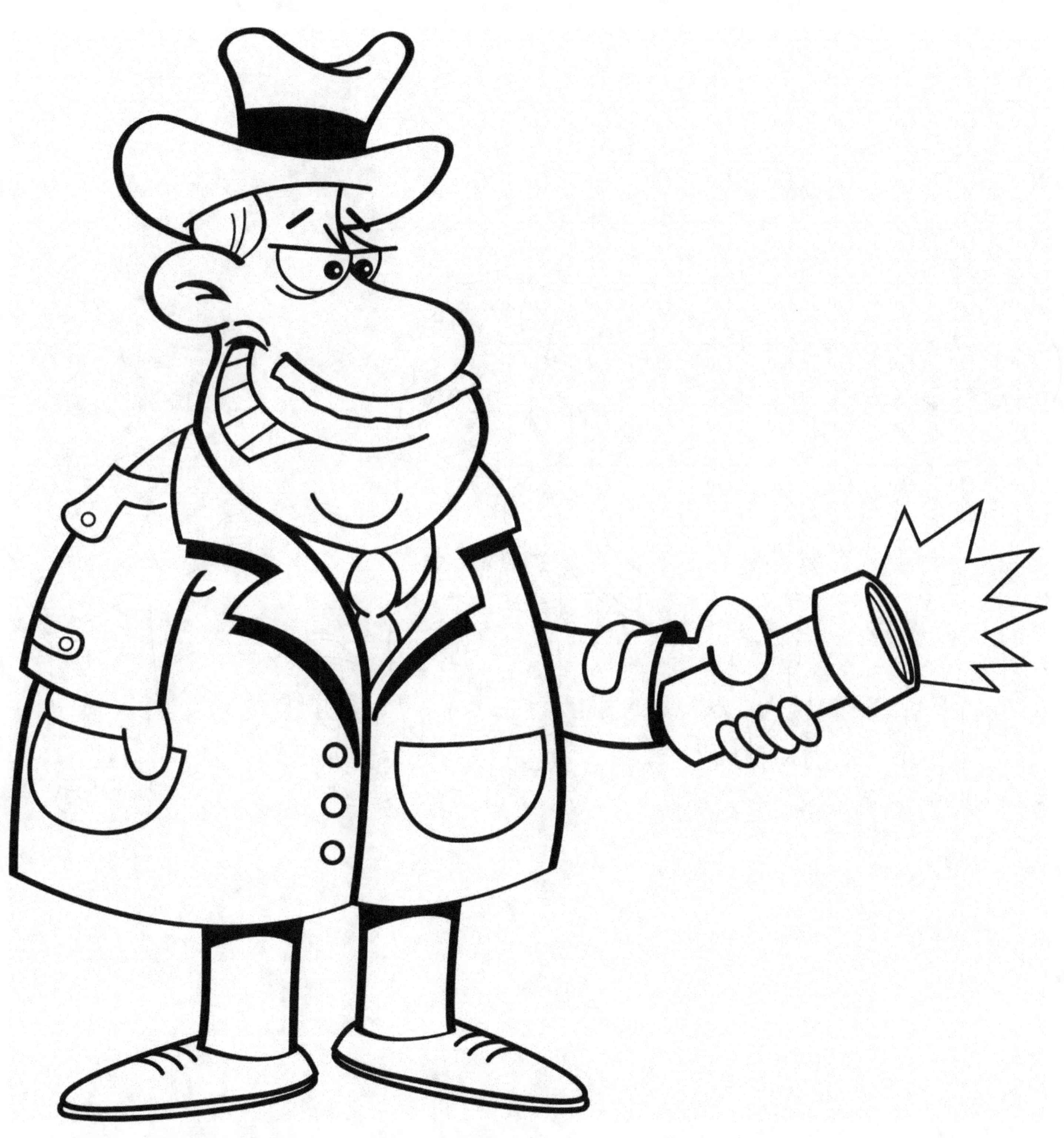

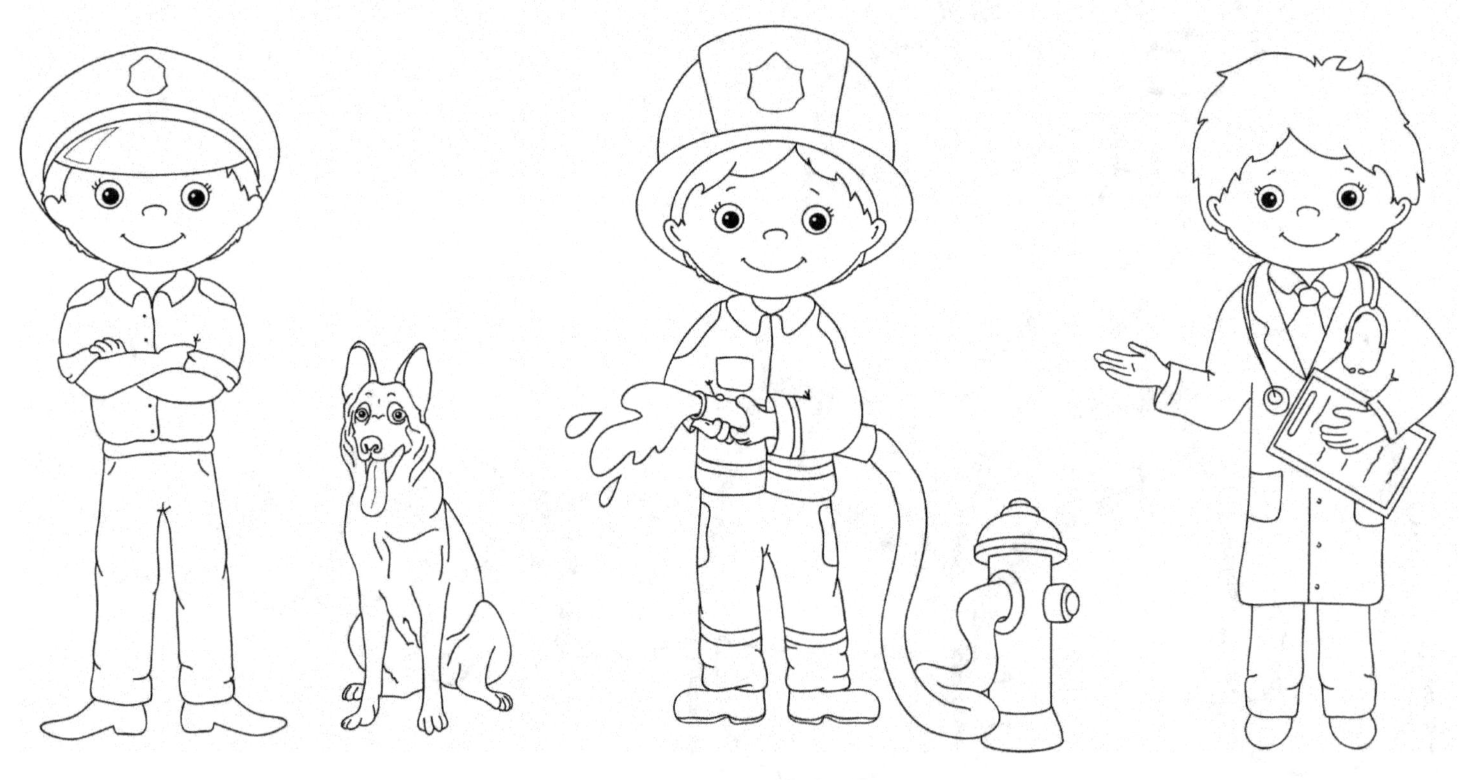

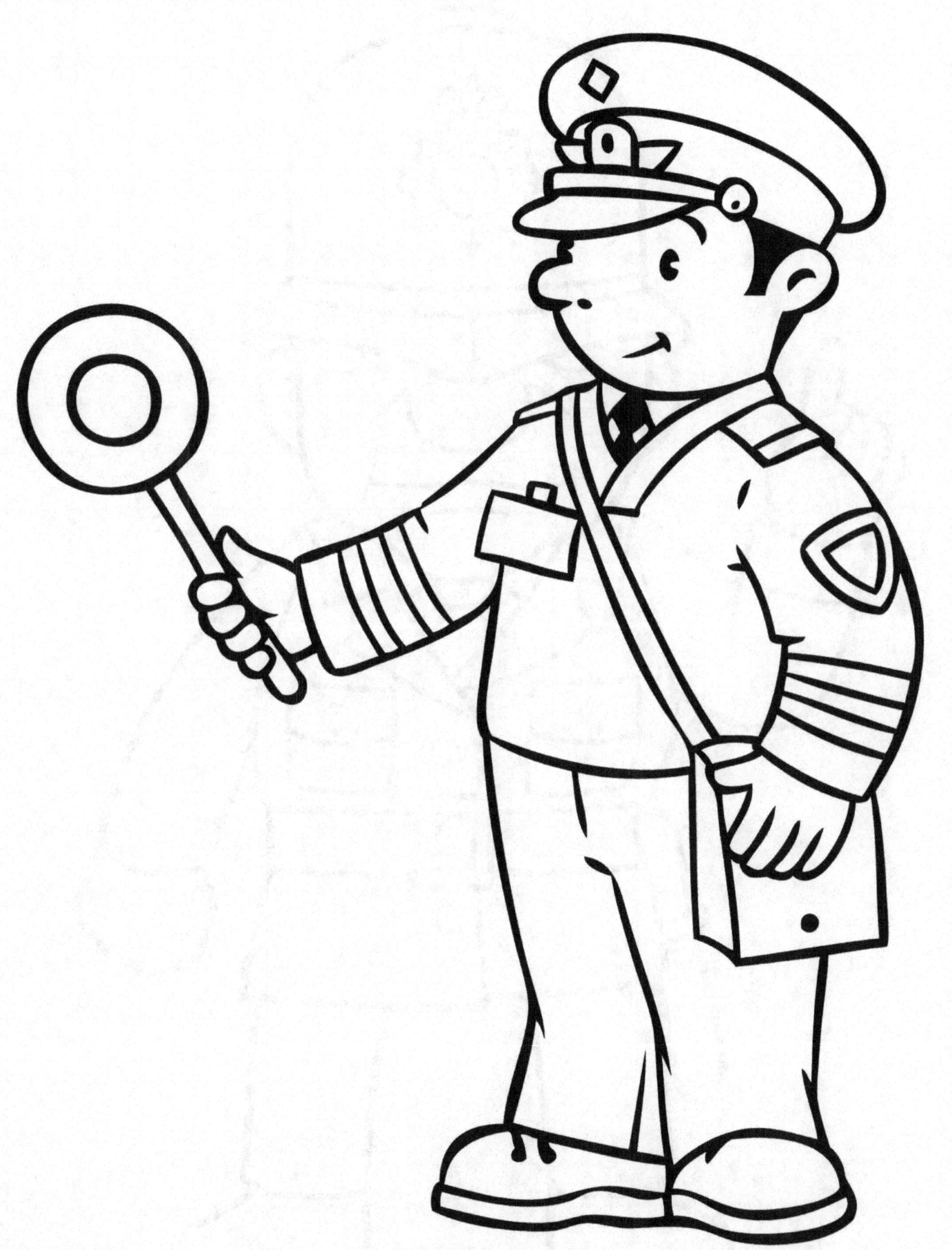

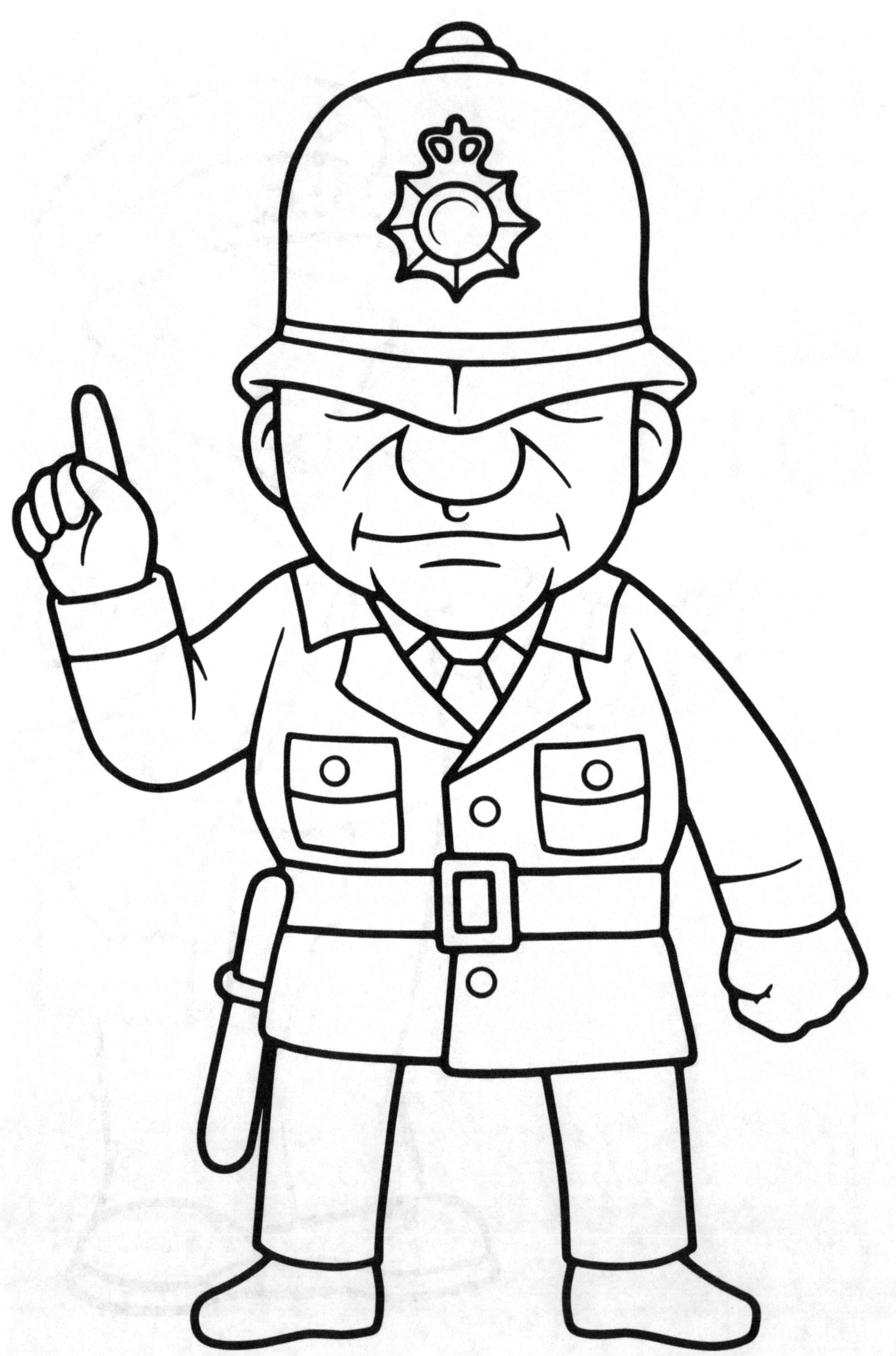

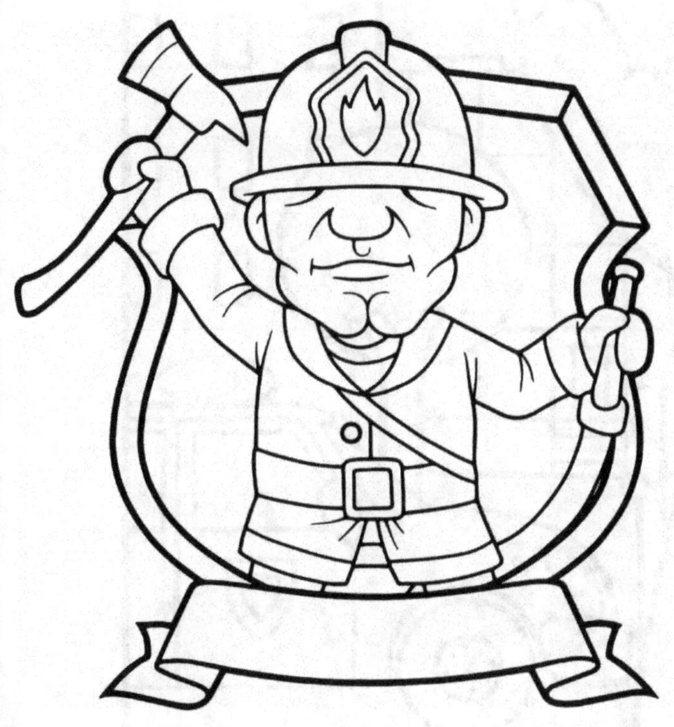

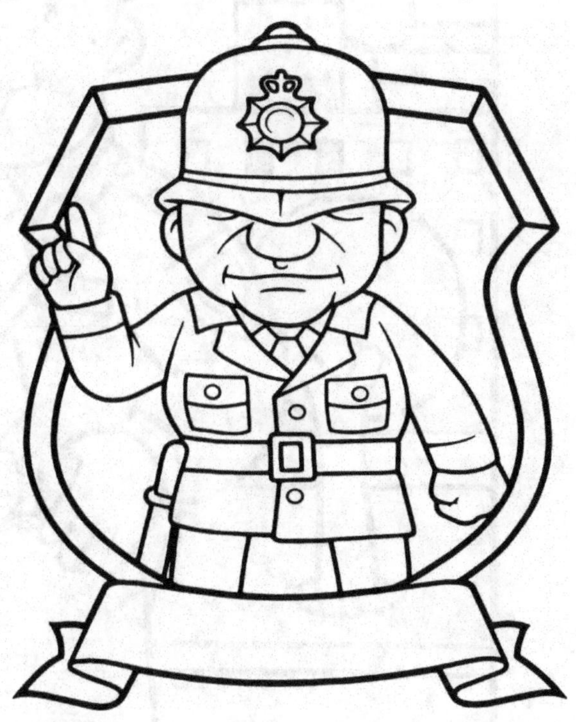

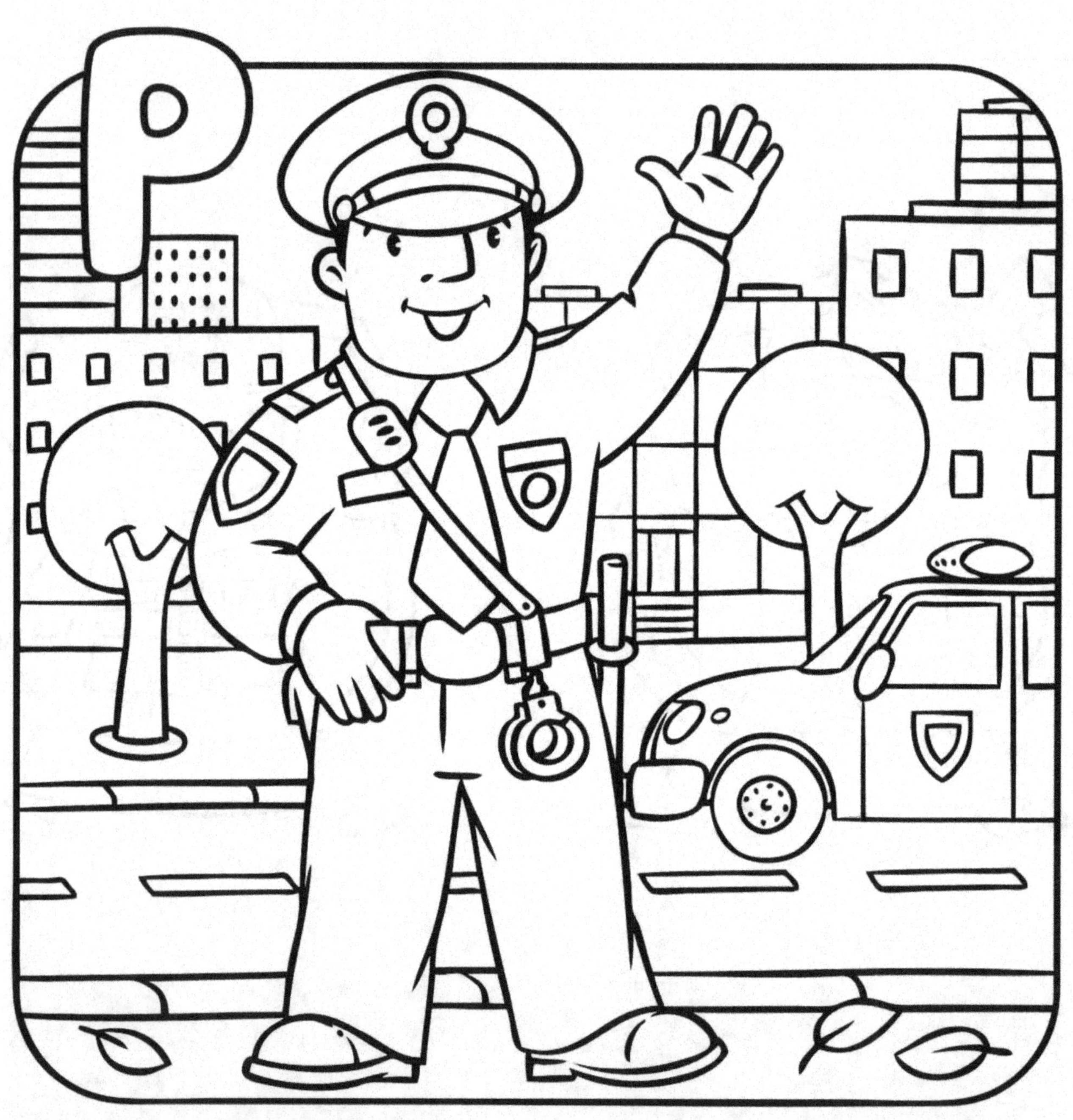

P

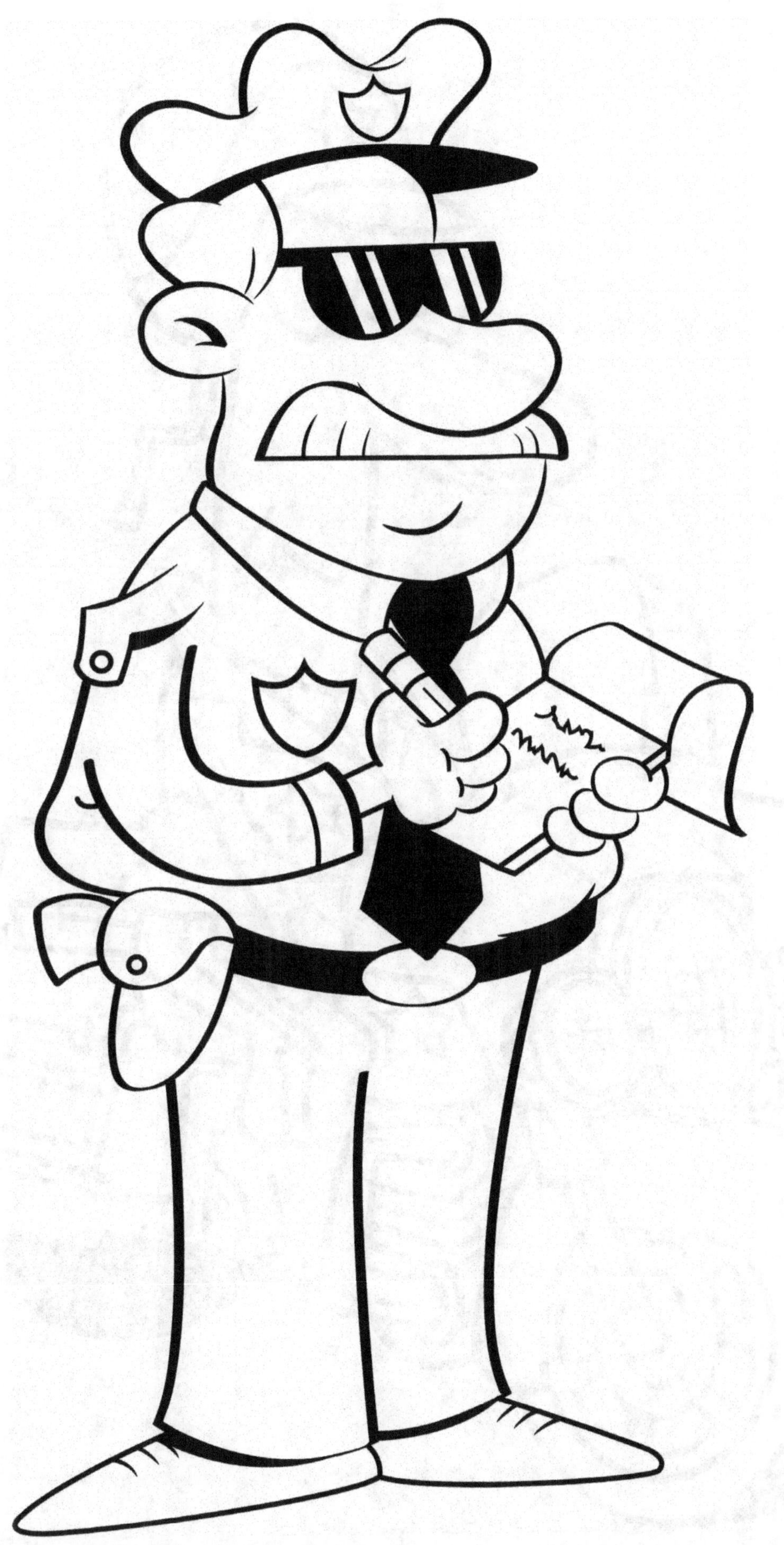

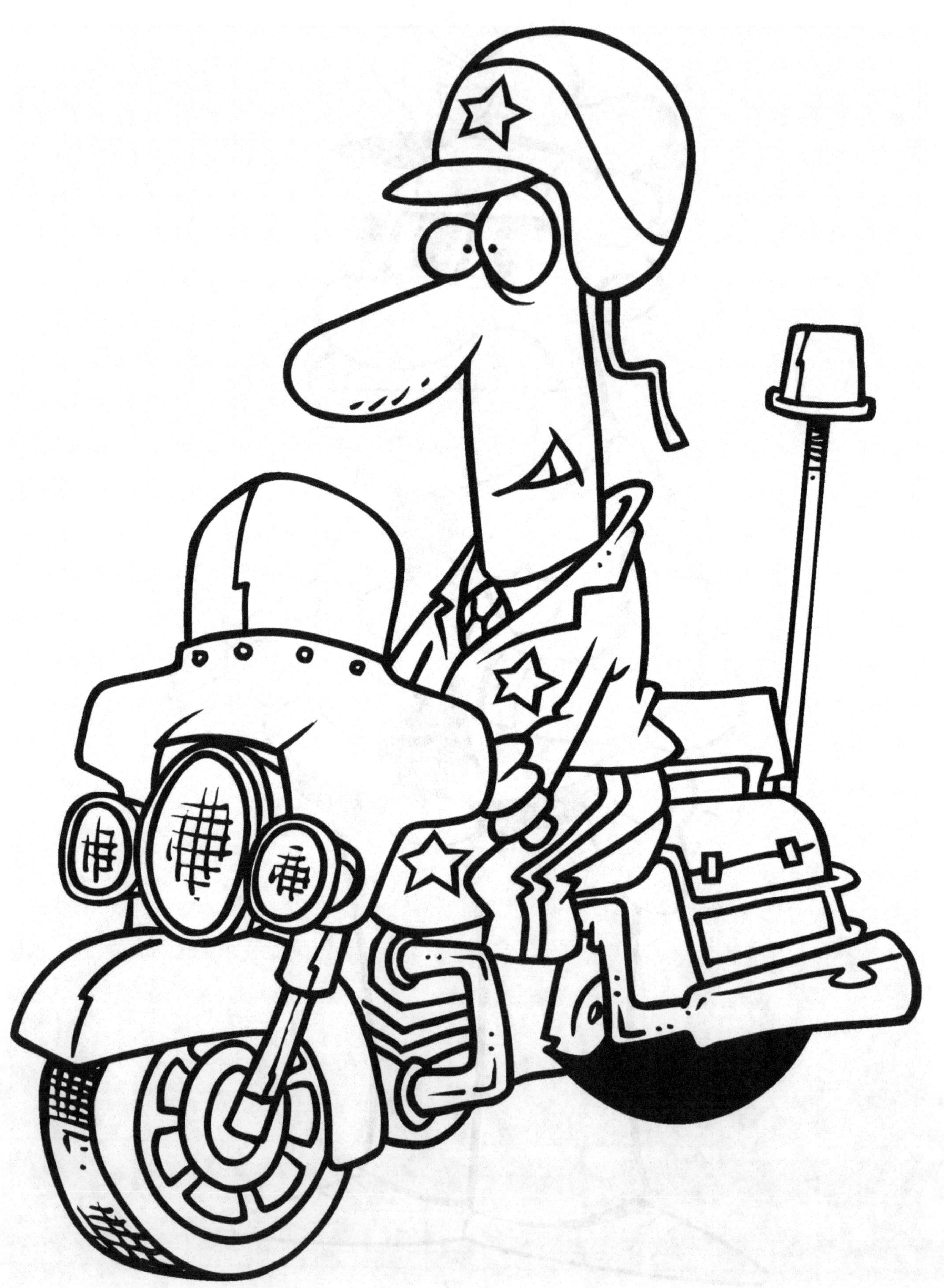

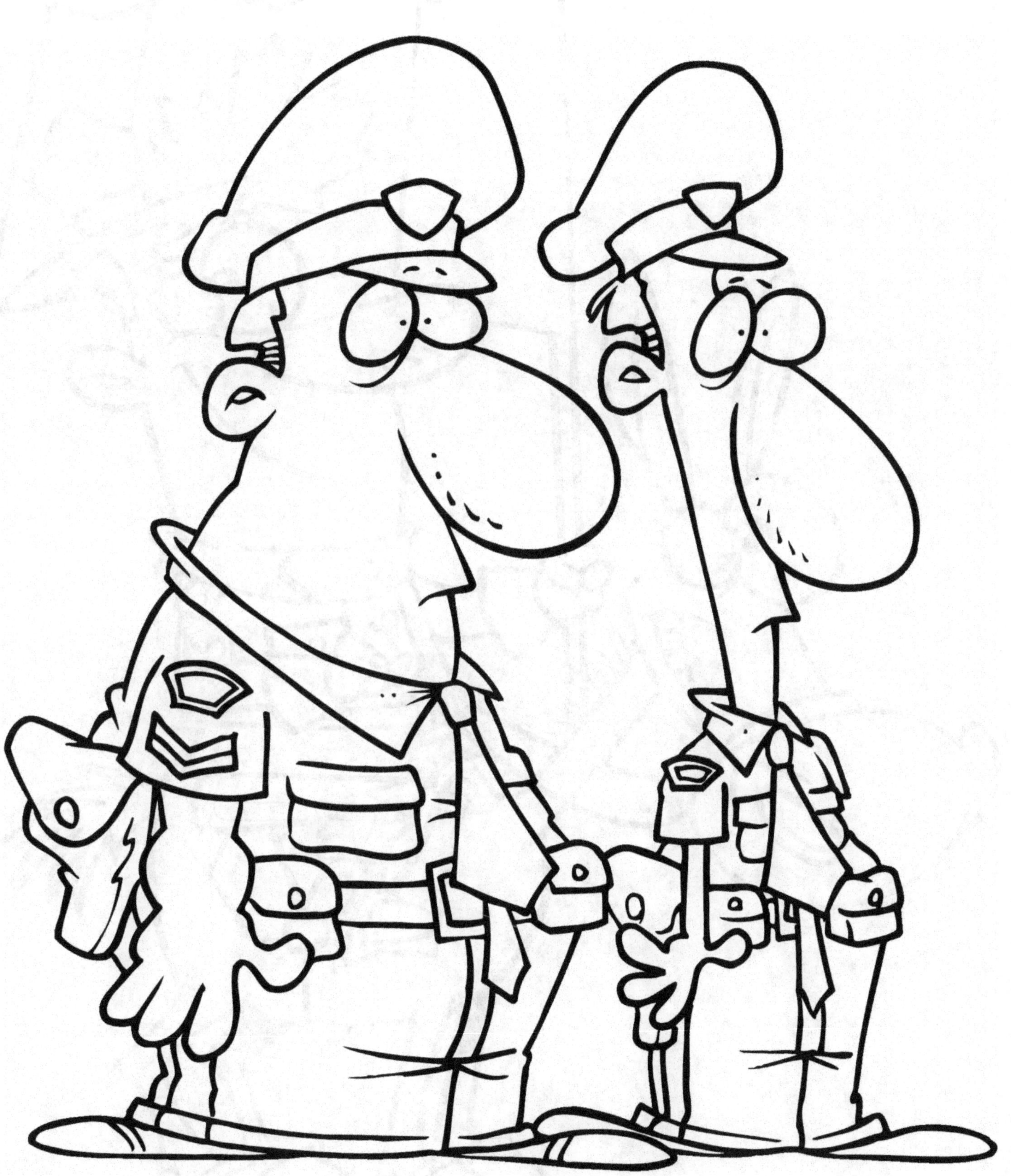

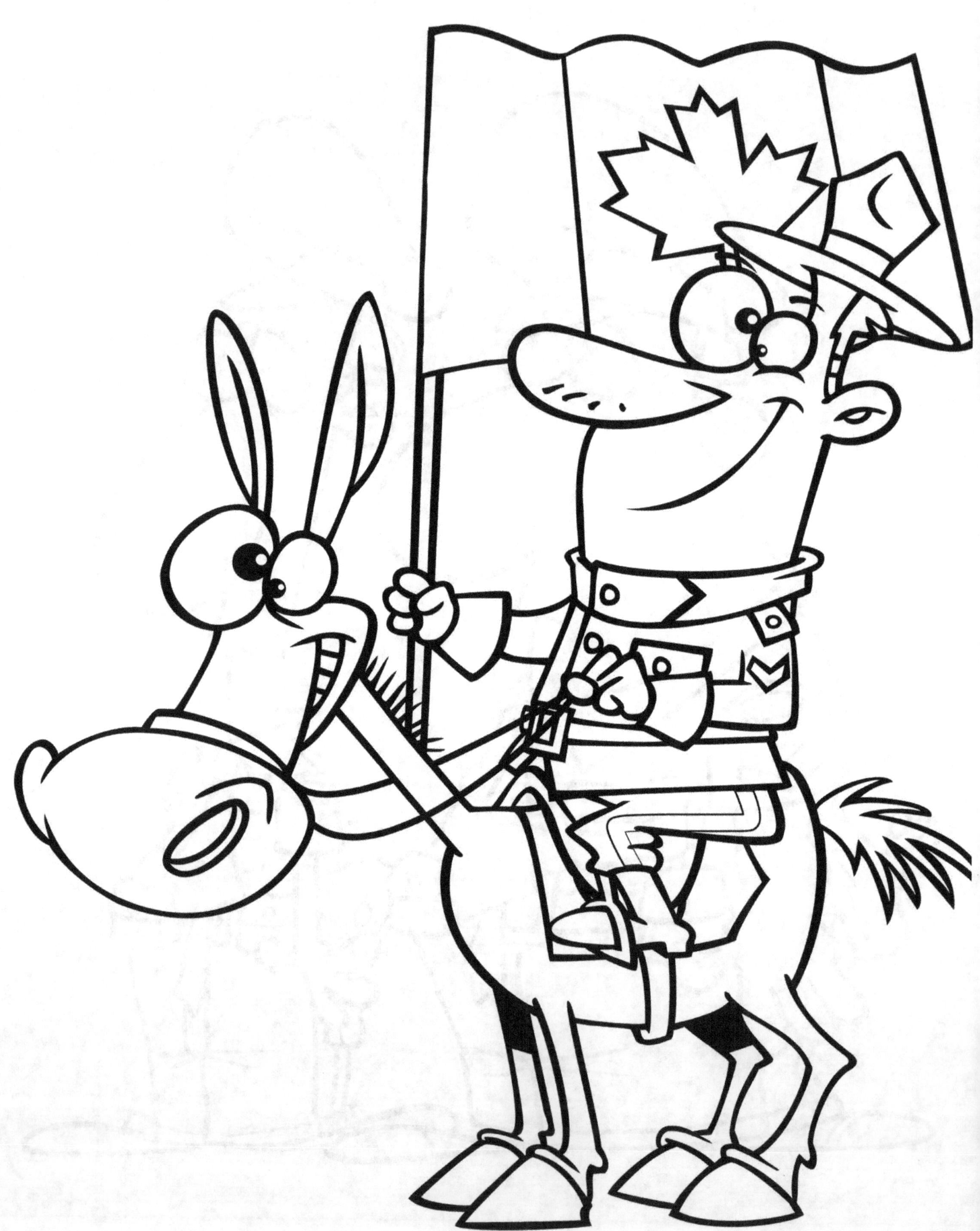

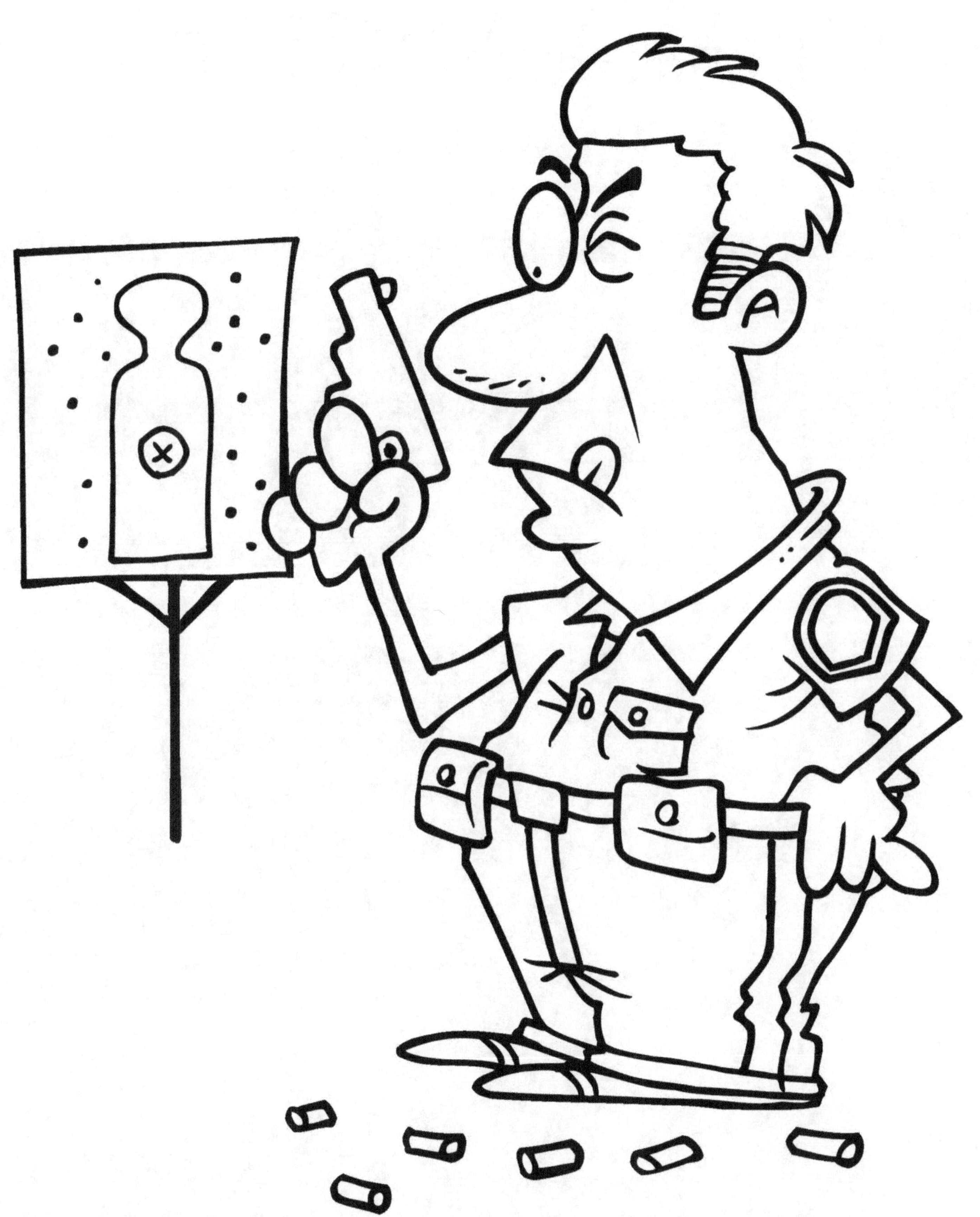

www.ingramcontent.com/pod-product-compliance
Lightning Source LLC
Chambersburg PA
CBHW082243060726
47598CB00016B/2759